THE $1K INVESTOR

SIMPLE, SMART STEPS TO START INVESTING WITH $1K OR LESS

BY

DEBBIE SASSEN

Disclaimer:

The information contained in this book is intended to be an introduction to many of the important and foundational topics related to investing and saving. It is not intended to be a substitute for personalized advice from financial, legal and tax professionals. I have made every effort to keep the information current and accurate. However, since financial market conditions and legal and tax considerations can change, no guarantee can be made as to the accuracy of the information contained within.

Dedication:

To my husband Jonathan who walks by my side
with love, wisdom, and support.

Contents

Introduction

Have you always believed investing was for *other* people?

If you're like many professional women with whom I work in my Financial Planning and Coaching practice, the idea of investing is scary.

Stories of stock market crashes or that friend who put everything into a hot tip that turned sour can leave you wanting to play it safe. After all, why take the risk of investing when you can safely 'grow' your money in a savings account?

Then there are the messages we internalize from society like "money management is a complicated minefield that's best left to the professionals."

Or perhaps you're so busy earning a living and looking after your family that investing for the future keeps taking a back seat to more immediate concerns.

If any of this resonates for you, I can relate

Looking at my life now, you might assume I've always known what I was doing around money. Even sixteen years ago - when I was at the peak of my high-powered, 23-year investment banking career, advising multi-national companies and governments how to manage their wealth - you might have thought I was completely on top of my own finances.

And if you'd asked me at the time, I'd probably have told you that I thought I was pretty money-savvy. Unfortunately, the truth isn't nearly as flattering as that.

It took a crisis to show me what was really going on

You see, sixteen years ago, my husband was diagnosed with cancer. Thank G-d he's healthy now - but at the time, not surprisingly, it was a difficult, emotionally worrying period for our family. And on top of that, I also learned that I was much less 'together' around my family's finances than I'd thought.

As we scrambled to adjust to this curveball life had thrown us, I discovered that even though I was a financial professional who understood the jargon, I hadn't been acting like one in my personal finances. For example:

- I'd barely made time to look over my financial paperwork and statements as they'd come in each month.
- When the HR department had sent me the documents for my retirement package, I'd just added them to my ever-growing 'to-do' pile to check out later (but never did).
- And when I'd finally bitten the bullet and decided it was time to start investing, I'd simply brought in an investment manager without asking many questions about his fees and how he operated.

As a result, I was pretty clueless about how my money was being invested and what I could expect for our financial future.

During my personal financial awakening, I discovered that a significant amount of our investment returns had been eroded by the investment manager's exorbitant fees. Not only that, but his standard operating procedure also involved regular buying and selling of the investments in our account (called 'churning') - which increased his commission, and skimmed the cream off the top of our returns.

So instead of building wealth to protect our family's future, my 'smart investing' was making *him* rich.

You don't need to wait for a crisis to take charge

My husband's diagnosis forced me to face the areas in which I hadn't been taking responsibility with our family's finances. It's pretty embarrassing that, despite all my years of high-powered financial career experience, I'd made so many mistakes. And more than that, I was angry - at the investment manager, and also at myself.

In that moment, I vowed that this was the point it all changed. *This* was the moment I started getting truly money-smart. I took the steps you'll read about in this book, and I began to turn things around.

And having now worked with hundreds of women who've started in a similar place in their financial affairs, I know it's pretty common for the trigger that prompts financial change to be some kind of crisis or upheaval.

But I want you to know that it doesn't have to be.

Going through a crisis - be it a health scare, the death of a loved one, a lost job or a major relationship breakup - is traumatic enough on its own. Discovering a bunch of financial issues that crop up because you haven't been paying attention is one more thing to deal with - and at the worst possible time.

I pray that you don't wait for a crisis to jolt you into taking charge of your money.

You also don't need to be super-rich to start investing

One of the most damaging assumptions about investing I see is that it's only for the super-wealthy. People assume that they can't even think about investing until they have tens of thousands of dollars at their disposal.

The reality is actually the reverse. If you do it right, investing is what allows you to grow your wealth over time so that you'll have *hundreds* of thousands of dollars.

You can start investing with as little as a thousand dollars - thus the name of this book. In fact, the truth of the matter is that you can start with even less. And little by little, if you manage your money properly, it will grow.

This book is for everyone who believes that investing is 'too complicated'

As I started taking responsibility for our finances, I realized that making smart investments that would provide for my family's future was actually pretty simple.

I started teaching my step-by-step process to other women (and men) and saw them getting great results. But not everyone can work one-on-one with me, or attend one of my workshops. That's why I decided to write the process down and make it accessible to one and all.

That's where the book you're holding in your hand (or viewing on your screen) came from. I wrote it for you and for everyone else who believes that investing is too hard, too complex or too dangerous. For everyone who believes that investing isn't for them because they're not mega-rich.

On some level, I wrote it for my younger self in the years before my husband's diagnosis. I wrote it for the Debbie who was so caught up in managing finances for her corporate clients that she neglected the *far-more-important-to-her* finances for her family.

And yes, if you want to avoid making the mistakes that that 'younger Debbie' made, I wrote it for you too. I wrote it to help you build both your family's future, and your sense of confidence and empowerment around money.

I really hope you find it useful.

With dear blessings for your investing success,

Debbie xo

SECTION 1

WHAT YOU NEED TO KNOW BEFORE YOU USE THE STEP-BY-STEP PROCESS

Chapter 1
Investing is MUCH Simpler than You Think

Why investing feels so intimidating

Money isn't easy to talk about at the best of times. Maybe you grew up with parents who struggled financially - so investing wasn't even on their radar. Or perhaps your parents fought bitterly about money, so you learned that it was a dangerous subject and a source of anxiety. Or maybe your parents learned from their own parents that 'religion, politics and money' were best avoided in polite company - so now you don't talk about money, either.

Add to this the fact that, for many women, the word 'investing' brings to mind the image of a condescending financial advisor or banker in a sharp suit. They imagine him sitting in his cold, shiny office behind his huge mahogany power-desk, smiling like a shark while not-so-secretly judging them for their lack of knowledge.

It might also bring to mind an endless stream of jargon and industry terminology - assets, shares, stocks, bonds, profit margins, dividends... and that's before you start getting into all the abbreviations.

Regardless - unless you've grown up in a family that was both money-smart AND that talked transparently about financial matters, money can feel like a simmering cauldron of stress. And when it comes to even the *idea* of investing, you can end up feeling completely overwhelmed.

It's actually simple - and it's essential

But, as I mentioned in the introduction, investing can be much simpler than we think. You can *absolutely* learn what you need to know to make smart investing decisions - and you'll find most of what you need to know in this book.

As a comparison, before my husband's cancer diagnosis, I had no idea about the different kinds of cancer that existed, and all the terminology around it. After he was diagnosed though, I quickly learned about different types of cancer cells, staging, and neoplasm.

I believe that all it takes to understand the terminology around investing is to have someone sit down with you and explain it - without making you feel incompetent for not already knowing it.

And I also think that understanding financial terminology helps you make good money management decisions for your family.

So that's what I want this book to do for you - I want you to discover with delight that you're totally capable of mastering investing.

Good investment decisions get you more than just money

I don't want to downplay the importance of creating a secure financial future for your family. Granted, as a Financial Planner and Money Coach, I'm biased on that front: I believe it's one of the greatest gifts you can give them.

That said, getting money-wise can give you so much more than financial success - I see it as the ultimate in self-care for you too. Taking care of your money and growing your wealth means less stress and worry for you. It means you can relax, be at peace and get on with your life. You'll enjoy an expansive energy that filters out into all the other areas of your life.

Plus, there's a confidence that comes with understanding exactly where you are now financially, where you're going, and how you'll get there. That confidence allows you to walk tall. You'll interact differently with people, and bring your full heart and soul to whatever you do.

When you have a strong, secure safety net underneath you, you'll feel more comfortable taking intelligent, considered risks. You won't hold yourself back from trying new things out of a fear of what might happen -

either on the money front, or anywhere else in your life.

And when you're no longer stressing about money, you can serve in the way you want to serve - whether that's serving your family, your community, or the world as a whole. You can give generously to the causes you care about, and support the businesses and providers you believe in. You can be a source of positive change in the world in a way that's just not possible when some part of you is constantly worrying about your family's financial future.

Making the mindset shift to being an investor

So how do you make the mindset shift from being someone who gets intimidated by financial planning to being an investor? It takes three steps.

1. Be aware of the influence of your past

First, take a step back and look at your early money history. Ask yourself what you learned from your parents and from the world around you about money. What beliefs about money do you carry now that could sabotage you on your journey to becoming a smart investor? (Note: you can download bonus material and worksheets at https://debbiesassen.com/bookbonuses/.)

- Did you grow up hearing that there was never enough - or that your family were spenders, not savers?
- Did your parents constantly tell you they couldn't afford things - or perhaps they regularly splurged on luxury gifts to fill other needs they weren't meeting?
- Did you absorb messages about rich people being selfish and greedy, or that money was the root of all evil?

Critically examine the messages you absorbed in your childhood and teenage years. Ask yourself whether they're always true, and look for real-life examples that contradict them.

2. Recognize that everyone needs to learn about money

You're not alone in needing to *learn* how to invest. None of us popped out of our mothers' wombs knowing how to manage an investment portfolio. Yes, some people have a greater aptitude for numbers and financial concepts, so they pick it up more easily than others... but it's not rocket science.

If you can find someone who's willing to explain this stuff to you in your own language, you'll probably find yourself looking back and wondering why it ever seemed so complicated in the first place.

3. Realize that even the best people make mistakes

Finally, remember that wherever you are financially right now, it's OK. And you're probably not the first person to be in that position. If you're worried that you've totally messed up your finances or that you've left it too late to start taking control, I want to reassure you that many people before you have started here too.

Someone, somewhere has been where you are now... and has turned things around for themselves and their family. For example, one of my worst mistakes back before I got smart about investing involved a 'sure thing' investment that ended up losing over $50,000. It was a really dumb mistake - especially from someone who'd worked in one of the biggest investment banks on Wall Street.

It would have been easy to sit back, wring my hands and say, "That proves it. I'm hopeless with managing my own money." But instead, I chose to regroup, move forward, and learn enough that I never made the same mistake again. And *that's* why I am where I am today.

So trust me when I say that it IS possible.

Action steps

Take out your journal (or just open a file on your computer) and answer the following questions:

1. What messages do you remember absorbing as a child or young adult about money and wealth? How might these messages affect your decision to get money-smart?

2. What things can you do easily now that you started off being bad at, and had to learn how to do over time? Can you imagine getting financially smart as being the same?

3. What mistakes have you made in the past with money? Write them down, forgive yourself for them, and decide that today you start learning how not to repeat them.

Download your free worksheets at
https://debbiesassen.com/bookbonuses/.

Chapter 2
Can you REALLY invest
with just $1,000?

You don't need millions of dollars to get started

In Chapter 1, I mentioned the image of a financial advisor 'shark' that investing brings to mind for many women. Of course, it's not always true (for a start, I don't even *own* a mahogany power desk) - but believing it, even just a little bit at a subconscious level, can keep you from taking action.

Another mistaken impression about investing that all too many people hold is that it's only possible to get going if you have a large amount of cash - five, six or even seven figures' worth of money. So if you don't have a chunk of change sitting around doing nothing - an inheritance or a redundancy payout, for example - you might figure that it's not worth even learning about investing.

Now it's true that some of my clients *did* suddenly find themselves with sums of money that they didn't know what to do with. Others were professionals or businesswomen who'd developed good saving practices over time - then looked up to discover that they'd built up a very healthy savings balance. They came to me because they suspected on some level that the money in their account could be working much harder for them than it was.

But I've also worked with many people who started with only a small amount of money. They had a thousand dollars, maybe two... and then followed the steps you'll learn in this book to gradually, over time, add to it and grow it into something that would provide for them and their families in the future.

So if the key to investing isn't actually what you start off with, what is it?

The real key is consistency

The reason so many people think you need 'big bucks' to get started is that they believe investing is a one-off action you take. This seems to be the version of investing we see most often in movies and the media.

In this version, you start with a windfall, invest it into something with high returns, ignore it until it's time to sell... and then discover with delight that you've made back many times the amount of your initial investment.

But nothing could be further from the truth. Instead, you need to start where you are and consistently take small action steps. If you don't have $1,000 right now, save up $100 a week (or even $100 a month, if that's your financial reality) until you do.

Invest that $1,000 using the steps outlined in Section 2 of this book, and continue investing consistently. Then add a fixed sum to your investments at the end of every month.

In this way, your investments will grow steadily over time.

The results of consistency in action

Natasha (Tash) Corbin, business strategist and entrepreneur, was a student in my online program *Smart Women Build Wealth*. She could absolutely see the benefits of investing and wanted to get started - but she wasn't able to save even $100 each month.

So Tash made the executive decision to start where she was. She committed to putting aside $2 a day; and for a while, that was all she could manage. As she put it, "Even I don't miss $2 a day." Then, over time she increased that amount - first to $3, then $5, then $10... and today's she's setting aside $25 a day!

Now $25 a day is around $750 a month. If you'd asked Tash back when she started whether she thought she'd *ever* be able to afford to save $750 a month, she'd have laughed in disbelief. Not only that, she would have said, "In my family the money message was *we're spenders, not savers*." But over time, Tash found ways to free up that money - buying less of the things she didn't really need, making fewer unplanned purchases and generally being more conscious and mindful in her spending. Plus, she focused on increasing her income to turbocharge her investing.

After 11 months, Tash had built up over $3,000 in her investment account. Plus, more than just having that money, she'd also developed consistent saving and investing habits that meant her $3,000 was only the beginning.

Today, nearly two years after joining *Smart Women Build Wealth*, Tash has increased her investment account well beyond $3,000. She feels in control of her finances and her life in a way she really never did before - bringing with it that sense of confidence and competence we talked about in Chapter 1.

Action steps

If you don't have $1,000 right now, go back through your last three months of bank statements and ask yourself:

1. What purchases have I made over the past few months that haven't really felt like "value for money" after I'd bought them?
2. What subscriptions do I have that I no longer use or could downgrade to a more basic option? What unnecessary fees am I paying that I could reduce?
3. Based on your answers to the above questions, ask yourself 'how much can I realistically save each month (or week, or day) to put towards an investment?'

NOTE: this is not about making yourself miserable, or sacrificing things that are really important to you or that give you genuine pleasure. Rather, it's about looking at your 'leaks' - the things you're spending money on that AREN'T really adding value to your life.

Download your free worksheets at
https://debbiesassen.com/bookbonuses/.

Chapter 3
It Starts with Saving
(but it doesn't end there)

The difference between saving and investing

Many people use the words 'saving' and 'investing' interchangeably - and it's true that both require setting aside money for the future. Both also involve choosing to forgo spending money on something today so you can get more value from that money in the long term.

But, at least for financially savvy people, that's where the similarity ends. When you save money, you put it aside - ideally in an interest-bearing account - and leave it there. This has some advantages like easy accessibility in the case of an emergency or for known upcoming expenses, but it's a not a great long-term investment strategy. We'll talk about why later in this chapter.

When you *invest* money, however, you make it actively work for you. You invest in something that you expect will give you higher returns than a savings account - and which will create those returns over a longer period of time (generally around five to ten years, or more).

Because each option - saving and investing - has its own benefits and drawbacks, you need both. Let's start with saving.

Why saving is non-negotiable

In the last chapter, you learned that it's possible to start investing, even with a small amount of money, by consistently setting aside sums and letting them grow. But regardless of whether you start with a lump sum or with small, consistent additions to your investments, you still need to *save* money.

Why? Because savings enable you to cover the unexpected expenses and little emergencies that *always* happen in life - things like dental work, a broken washing machine, pet care and car repairs, to name just a few - without jeopardizing your investments.

Plus, investing needs time. It requires patience to sit on the sidelines while your money is busy growing. It also requires discipline to hold onto your investments without selling out too early when the financial markets are crashing. One of the biggest reasons that sensible people (i.e. those who *don't* invest in get-rich-quick schemes, and do almost everything else right) lose money on investments is that they sell them before they'd planned to. This usually happens because they either need the money, or they panic when the financial markets drop.

A good savings cushion means you can leave your investments alone and just let them do their thing.

The two types of saving

To set yourself up in a way that covers you regardless of what life throws at you, I recommend creating two separate savings accounts.

- **A 'periodic needs' savings account** for irregular expenses that don't happen every month, but which you know to expect. These expenses might include school fees for your children, car maintenance and your summer vacation.

- In each of these situations, you know the expense will be coming up. If you diligently save a little from each paycheck, the money will be there for you when you need it. Finance guru Dave Ramsey[1] calls this a 'Sinking Fund'.

- **An 'emergency needs' savings account** for the kind of unexpected expenses that always arise in the course of the year. Of course, you hope you won't need to tap in-

---

[1] https://www.daveramsey.com/.

to your emergency savings account, but it's reassuring to know the money is there 'just in case'. Emergencies can be something small like an air conditioning repair, something bigger like losing your job, or - G-d forbid - being diagnosed with a serious illness as my husband was.

Dave Ramsey calls this type of saving your 'Emergency Fund'. He recommends starting out with $1,000 saved up in your Emergency Fund, and then building up enough over time to cover your living expenses for three to six months.

Personally, I like to call this the Financial Freedom Fund. You'll feel true financial freedom when money is there, stress-free, exactly when you need it most.

Everybody's situation is different. So figure out how much money you need in each of these accounts - **then keep them topped up!** Make sure to replenish your accounts every time you withdraw money from them. That way, you know you'll never have to sell an investment early to cover a flat tire, a broken washing machine, or x-rays for your dog.

But saving alone isn't enough

While saving helps you to cover short-term spending needs, it's a poor strategy for creating long-term wealth. The primary reason is that the interest rates on savings accounts are usually lower than inflation (the tendency of prices to rise over time). A lesser, but still important, reason is taxes. Since savers in most countries pay taxes on the interest they earn, their *after-tax* interest rate is even lower than the one their bank advertises.

Taken together, inflation and taxes are likely to create a situation in which the number in your savings account goes up over time, while your *purchasing power* (the amount of goods and services you can buy with your money) goes down.

That's why saving money is not a long-term investment strategy. If you want to grow your money, you do need to do something more.

Action steps

1. Start by saving $1,000 in your Emergency/Financial Freedom account. Then skip to Step 2 below. Once you have your periodic spending needs covered, decide how many months' worth of living expenses you'd need to cover yourself in an emergency.

2. Deposit a little bit from each from paycheck into this account.

3. Next, review your bank statements for the last twelve months. Make a note of the periodic expenses you've had that you can reasonably expect to have again in the future.

Calculate the total you need and start putting a little money aside from each paycheck into your Periodic Savings account. Remember to top the account back up after each withdrawal.

4. Once you have enough money in both of these savings accounts, you're ready to start investing.

Download your free worksheets at: https://debbiesassen.com/bookbonuses/.

Chapter 4
Investment Options Demystified

The four most common types of investments

There are many investment options - an almost unlimited number of them, in fact. From companies to land to wine to precious metals to government bonds to art, stamps or coins - almost *anything* you can buy for one price and sell for another can be called an 'investment'.

However, four of the most common investment options are:

- Property (real estate)
- Stocks and shares
- Bonds
- Mutual funds and ETFs (Exchange Traded Funds)

These investment options are easily accessible; and with the exception of real estate, they can be bought and sold (i.e. traded) on public exchanges.

In this chapter, I'll cover each of these options, including their benefits and drawbacks.

Property (real estate)

Property is probably the easiest option for non-financial people to understand. After all, we know what property is. We can see it, touch it and feel it. It's tangible. And most of us live in a house or apartment, whether we own it or rent it from someone who owns it.

So it's easy to grasp that by either renting a property out, or buying it at one price and selling it at a higher one (or both), there's an opportunity to make money. In fact, many people only feel comfortable investing in real estate - even though it might not be the right choice for everyone. We'll talk about why in Chapter 9.

Benefits of investing in property

- It's widely available.
- There are many alternatives available, including apartments, houses, apartment complexes, office buildings, store fronts, shopping malls, parking lots and more.
- There's the potential for a high return on your investment.
- You can use *leverage,* which means you can invest a small amount of money and borrow the rest to buy a large property. For example, you can invest $20,000 in a $100,000 property by borrowing $80,000 from the bank. The bank loan is called a mortgage.
- You can earn a consistent, steady stream of income from rent.
- There may be tax advantages in your state or country for mortgage payments and other expenses.
- You can use property to diversify your wealth if, say, most of your money is held in retirement accounts that own stocks and bonds.

Drawbacks of investing in property

- It may require a significant 'investment' of your time to source suitable properties and manage them.
- It requires a deep understanding of the expected future cash flows of the property to accurately predict the rate of return.
- You may have to invest time and money in the maintenance and upkeep of your property.
- Long periods of time without a tenant can significantly reduce your income and rate of return.
- You need a large sum of money to get started even if you borrow from the bank with a mortgage.
- Money invested in a single property is not diversified (we'll talk more about this later in this chapter). That's called putting all your eggs in one basket. A safer way to invest is to spread out your eggs.

- You generally can't sell a property quickly if you need cash. And if you're pressured to sell, you may have to reduce your price significantly.

Stocks and shares

Also called 'equity', a stock or share is a small ownership interest in a company. When you buy stock in a company like Coca-Cola, for example, you become a part-owner of the company. Even if the value of your stock amounts to one little brick in the wall of a bottling factory somewhere in the Far East, you still own it.

Stock prices rise and fall when investors perceive a change in the value of the company and/or in the overall direction of the financial markets. Sometimes, a stock's price fluctuates - i.e. rises and falls - to reflect real changes in the company, like when the release of a new iPhone goes gangbusters and the sales significantly increase Apple's profitability. At other times, the price changes because of expected changes in the economy. If the economy (either locally or globally) is growing and investors expect it to keep doing so, they believe that business will be good - so stock prices rise. If, on the other hand, they expect the economy to shrink, stock prices will drop in expectation of the decline.

When a company is profitable, it can choose to share those profits with the owners/investors by paying dividends. Many companies do pay dividends, but they aren't obligated to do so. When profits contract, a company may choose to reduce and even suspend dividend payments.

Benefits of investing in stocks

- You can purchase stocks easily through either a broker or an investment manager, or on your own.
- Stocks are an excellent way to grow your money over time and beat inflation.

- Investors have access to a wide variety of companies all over the world. Purchasing several different stocks makes it easy to create a diversified investment portfolio.
- Your stock portfolio doesn't take up space in your house, and you don't need to be on call 24/7 to manage it.
- You can easily take your stock portfolio with you if you move, because it stays where it is.
- Once you choose your investments, your money grows quietly in the background while you take care of the rest of your business and your life.

Drawbacks of investing in stocks

- Because stocks are so easy to buy, they're also easy to sell. Unfortunately, many investors quickly sell when there's panic in the financial markets, which locks in their losses.

- Choosing to invest in individual stocks requires an 'investment' of your time to find suitable companies and to monitor their progress.
- If you own stock in companies that run into financial difficulties and go bankrupt, you can lose all your money.

Bonds

A bond is similar to a loan. Sometimes, companies like Coca-Cola and governments like the United States need to borrow money to fund their projects and operations. These sums of money can be huge - in the hundreds of millions of dollars and beyond. One option is for these entities to borrow money from the bank.

Alternatively, the borrower can turn to a group of investors and take out a loan. In exchange for the loan, the borrower issues a promissory note - an I.O.U. - called a bond, which spells out the terms and conditions of the loan. The bond specifies:

- The amount of the loan, called the 'principal'.
- The term of the loan, e.g. five or ten years.
- The interest rate that the borrower is obligated to pay to the lenders, e.g. 3% or 5%.
- The frequency of the interest payments, e.g. once or twice yearly.

When the term of the loan finishes, the bond 'matures'. At that time, the borrower returns the principal to the lenders.

Benefits of investing in bonds

- Most bonds provide a steady, reliable stream of income for the term of the loan. A small subset of bonds pays a variable rate of interest or no interest at all, but I won't be discussing those in this book.
- If the borrower is an entity in good standing with a good credit rating, the likelihood that the bond will be paid back in full is very high. Formal credit rating

agencies like Moody's and Standard & Poor's assess the financial strength of borrowers and assign a rating that reflects their ability to make timely interest payments, and to pay back the loan.

- Due to their reliable payment stream, bond prices fluctuate less than those of stocks. As such, owning bonds as part of a diversified investment portfolio - one that includes bonds, stocks and other investments - helps to buffer extreme changes in the value of the overall portfolio, particularly during a financial market crisis.

- You can invest in a bond with a maturity date that roughly meets your need for cash. For example, if your son or daughter is planning on going to college in five years, you can buy a five-year bond.

- In the event of a financial emergency, you can sell most bonds quickly. The proceeds of the bond sale should be deposited in your account within a few days.

Drawbacks of investing in bonds

- The long-term expected return on a bond or bond portfolio is less than that of stocks and real estate. An investor with a long-term investment horizon of ten years or more is likely to be better off owning more stocks and real estate than bonds.

- When interest rates rise, the price of a bond drops, since the fixed interest rate on the bond is less attractive than it was 'yesterday'. If you wanted to sell your bond, you'd have to lower the price to entice someone to buy it.

The change in the price of the bond reflects the new reality in the financial markets. If you hold the bond to maturity (the end of the loan term) that shouldn't be a problem, since you'll get your money back. But if you need to sell the bond before it matures, you may get back less than you paid for it.

As you would expect, when interest rates fall the opposite happens - bond prices rise.

Mutual funds and ETFs (exchange traded funds)

For the purposes of this book, I'll group Mutual Funds and ETFs together by the more general name *funds*. Funds are a type of collective investment in which investors' money is pooled and used to purchase a variety of investment alternatives. The fund managers choose how to invest your money based on a set of investment goals and guidelines.

Some funds invest only in stocks. Others invest only in bonds. There are funds that invest exclusively in real estate or precious metals like gold. And some funds invest in a combination of different categories.

Since investments can be combined in an infinite number of ways, there are tens of thousands of funds available in the financial markets.

So how do you choose? How can you possibly know enough as a beginning investor to make the right choice?

Active vs. Passive Funds

Let's start by defining two different types of funds - actively managed funds and passively managed funds.

When a fund is managed actively, the investment manager (and their team) is constantly involved with the portfolio. And that makes sense - their job hinges on getting good returns for the people whose money they manage. They focus on the individual investments in the portfolio, asking:

- How are the funds doing relative to the market?
- Are the funds profitable?
- Are the funds generating the expected returns?
- Should they buy more, sell or hold on for a little longer?
- Do new opportunities exist that make more sense?

- Should they be adding new investments to the portfolio?

To help with this decision-making, the investment manager uses sophisticated computers and technological tools. They might even visit the companies in which they invest, or in which they're considering investing.

A passively managed fund, on the other hand, subscribes to a 'buy and hold' investment philosophy. The fund is designed to track or mimic the performance of a specific market as represented by a **market index**. The index is a measuring stick or a benchmark for how well the financial markets are performing (meaning whether they're gaining or losing, and by what percent).

A market index is created by combining several stocks (if you're creating a stock market index), or several bonds (for a bond market index). One well-known stock index is the Standard & Poor's 500 (S&P 500). This American index tracks the performance of 500 large companies whose stocks trade on the New York Stock Exchange or the NASDAQ: the second largest stock exchange in the world. The S&P 500 is widely used as a measure of general stock price levels in the United States.

A small sampling of stock market indexes around the globe includes the FTSE 100 in the UK, the ASX 200 in Australia and the Tel Aviv 125 in Israel.

Besides the difference in their investment philosophies, another big difference between actively and passively managed funds is their cost. Actively managed funds are labor-intensive, and fund managers charge high fees as a result. Passively managed funds, on the other hand, simply track the markets. The small number of computer-generated trades means that these funds can be less expensive. A second big difference is that over the long term, passively managed funds beat 80% of actively managed funds. In fact, a recent study shows that over a 15-year investment horizon, more than 90% of investment managers failed to beat the market[2].

---

[2] http://www.aei.org/publication/more-evidence-that-its-very-hard-to-beat-the-market-over-time-95-of-financial-professionals-cant-do-it/.

Benefits of investing in funds

* A financial expert pools together a group of investments, making it easy for you to create a diversified portfolio - either by owning a single fund or several funds.

- Sometimes, you can access certain investments that are only available to large investors via a fund.
- Creating a diversified portfolio with a small handful of funds is extremely cost-effective.

Drawbacks of investing in funds

- Both passive and active funds exist in the market and it's important to know the difference. An active mutual fund has an investment manager, or a team of investment managers, who make investment decisions for the fund.

  Those managers get paid by you, the investor, which reduces your returns. Additionally, while some investment managers *can* beat the market over short periods of time - and some can even beat the market over longer periods - it's impossible to know today who those managers will be.

- Rather than trying to "beat the market," a better goal is to match the market. You can do that by buying passive index funds that track the market. The fees on passively managed funds are extremely low because investments are generated by computer models and algorithms to exactly mirror the market.

Why it's so important to diversify

As I mentioned earlier, the prices of various investments like stocks, bonds, funds and real estate fluctuate over time. But they don't fluctuate by exactly the same magnitude at exactly the same time. In statistics, we say that they're not perfectly correlated. In everyday language, I like to say that some investments 'zig' while others 'zag'.

By creating a diversified portfolio and owning a variety of investments, you reduce the risk that the value of everything you own will drop at exactly the same time.

So instead of putting all your money in stocks (i.e. all your eggs in one basket), you invest some money in stocks, some in bonds and maybe some in property.

Similarly, when you buy a stock fund, rather than buying a single stock, you diversify the stock portion of your investment portfolio. That way, if a single company performs poorly and perhaps even goes bankrupt, the impact on your overall investment portfolio is minor. Of course, if your stock fund owns only a small amount of a company that has an amazing return (like Amazon in the last five years or Apple in the last ten years), the overall impact on your portfolio's performance will also be limited.

Diversification isn't a new idea

In the days of the Talmud 1,500 years ago, Rebbe Yitzchak said, "A person should divide his money into three: one third in land, one third in commerce, and one third at hand."[3,4]

I wouldn't advise taking this literally - the exact proportions that are right for you depend on your individual situation. But if you think of 'land' as referring to property, 'commerce' as referring to stocks and bonds, and 'money at hand' as easily accessible savings, the general principle holds true: diversify, diversify, diversify.

---

[3] http://www.aish.com/ci/be/88894267.html.
[4] https://www.businessinsider.com.au/the-talmud-strategy-2012-1.

Action steps

1. Ensure you're clear on the differences between property, stocks, bonds and funds, and the benefits and drawbacks of each.

2. Identify whether you need to learn more about any of them before you start to think about which ones are best for you and your family. If so, check out my online course *Investing Made Simple*, available through my website[5].

3. Make notes in your journal about the investment types you think are most appropriate for you and why. You don't have to do anything with these notes yet - they're just a record of your thought process at this point in your journey.

Download your free worksheets at https://debbiesassen.com/bookbonuses/.

---

[5] https://debbiesassen.com/.

SECTION 2

STEP-BY-STEP PROCESS

Chapter 5
Step 1 - Your 'Investing WHY' plus Setting Your Targets

Before you get started investing, you need to clarify *why* you want to invest.

I know I wrote earlier that investing is the best way to beat inflation and grow your wealth - and that's true. To enjoy those benefits, however, you have to be willing and able to invest for the long term. You need the fortitude to hold on to your investments when the market gets shaky and prices drop - which they will, as we'll talk about more later in the book. And if you're starting with only a small sum, you'll need to build wealth by continually adding more and more money to your investment portfolio.

As such, the more specific you can get about your goals - the more clarity you have about WHY you're investing in the first place - the more likely you are to stay the course and build wealth.

I don't think it's enough to say, "I want to be a millionaire." You might think that a million bucks will make you happy. But let's face it - there *are* miserable millionaires in the world. And some folks who hit millionaire status won't spend a dime because they're scared to let it go and shrink their wealth. On the other hand, many people of lesser means live lives filled with happiness, joy, meaning, wellness, and contentment.

So when you define your WHY, go deep. Get specific.

I like using SMART goals to do that. If you're not already familiar with the term, a SMART goal is:

- **S**pecific, not vague.
- **M**easurable, so you can gauge your progress, stay on track and rejoice when you reach your goal.

- **A**ttainable, given where you are now.
- **R**ealistic, which means you can reach it.
- **T**imely, so it has a specific deadline.

Here's an example of the difference between a fuzzy goal and a SMART goal:

- **Fuzzy Goal:** 'I want to be a millionaire.'
- **SMART Goal:** 'I want to have one million dollars in an investment account by the time I'm 65 so that I can retire without financial stress and worry, volunteer for causes that are important to me, and travel the world. I don't know what it will take to achieve that goal, but I'm committed to learning everything I can.

  In two months, I will have opened my first investment account and created a plan to regularly invest a fixed (to be determined) amount of money to reach my goal. I will review my goal every year on my birthday, and make any changes necessary to achieve it.'

See the difference?

When you know where you're going plus why you want to get there, you're much more likely to achieve your goals.

It's your turn now. Write down your investing WHY. Make sure to review it regularly.

How much money do you need your investments to make?

Let's start by trying to figure out how much money you're likely to need in the future. This can vary widely depending on your age and life situation. And I completely understand that the younger you are, the more challenging it will be to come up with a number. Nevertheless, your answer should be more specific than "as much as possible".

Just for today, choose a goal that sounds reasonable and makes sense to you.

Don't worry if it's not 'the' number. As you learn more about investing and become more confident, there'll be many opportunities to refine your goal.

Meanwhile, getting started sooner rather than later is a big part of your long-term investing success.

Identify when you'll need the money

Next, you need to know when you'll need the money from your investments. This will be different for everyone.

If you've just turned 30, you might not need to access your money until you retire in 30 or 40 years. Or perhaps you'll want a nest egg available in 20 or 25 years to give your children higher education, or help them put a down payment on their first property to launch them into adulthood.

If you're already retired, you might require some of your money to be accessible immediately (think savings), while other pots of money become available in five, ten, fifteen and even 30 years as you move through your senior years.

There are many options. The timeframe in which you'll need your money and how much you'll need will depend on a multitude of factors. These could include your other assets and sources of income like investment properties, pension plans and national insurance or social security.

The magic of compound interest

Albert Einstein called compound interest the eighth wonder of the world, famously saying that, "He who understands it earns it; while he who doesn't, pays it."

Compound interest happens when you constantly reinvest the interest you earn on your investments back into them. As a result, you earn interest on your interest. And then you earn interest on your interest on your interest. This process continues such that at the end of an extended period of time, your investments grow exponentially.

Let's see how that works out in the table below.

Year	Principal Sum	Interest Earned @10%	Total Value at Year-End
1	1,000	100	1,100
2	1,100	110	1,210
3	1,210	121	1,331
4	1,331	133	1,464
5	1,464	146	1,611
6	1,611	161	1,772
7	1,772	177	1,949
8	1,949	195	2,144
9	2,144	214	2,358
10	2,358	236	2,594

In this example, an investor starts by investing $1,000. This amount is called the **principal sum**. Assuming a 10% interest rate, she earns $100 in interest in her first year and ends up with $1,100 by the end.

At the beginning of her second year of investing, she reinvests the whole $1,100 and earns $110 in interest - $100 from her original $1,000 and $10 on the $100 interest. So by the end of year 2, the value of her investment has grown to $1,210.

In the third year, the cycle repeats itself. This time, the investor earns $100 on her original $1,000 investment and $21 on the interest on the interest. As the years pass and the process continues, she earns more and more of her return from compound interest. By the end of year 9, she earns more interest on the interest ($114) than she earned on her original $1000 investment.

This cycle of reinvesting interest and earning compound interest continues for ten years. At the end of that investment period, the interest earned has grown to $236 - more than double what it was in the first year. And the total investment equals $2,594 - a 259% increase in the principal sum.

That's the magic of compound interest; and I find it incredibly compelling.

Now let's see what happens when a young investor, whom we'll call Irene, starts investing at the age of 25. Irene consistently invests $100 every month until retirement at age 70.

Over time, she'll invest a total of $54,000 - 540 months (that's 45 years) x $100 each month = $54,000.

For this example, I'll use an 8% interest rate, which would be a reasonable long-term return on a diversified portfolio.

As you can see in the graph below, Irene's wealth grows to $502,000 over 45 years. Of that amount, only $54,000 is money she actively added to her investment. The remaining $448,000 is interest that she earned on her investment.

That mind-boggling number is the awesome magic of compound interest.

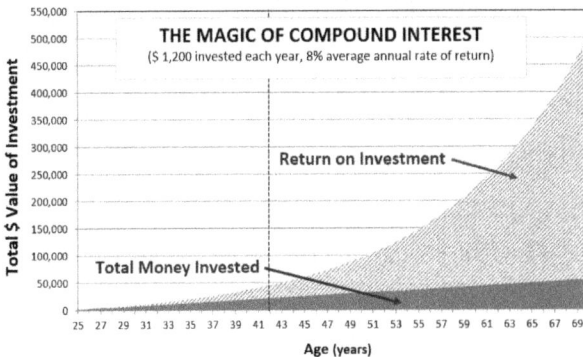

THE MAGIC OF COMPOUND INTEREST
($ 1,200 invested each year, 8% average annual rate of return)

Return on Investment

Total Money Invested

Total $ Value of Investment

Age (years)

The Rule of 72

A wonderfully useful and practical application of compound interest is **The Rule of 72**.

This clever little trick enables you to calculate how long it takes for your investments to double in value. If you have two investment alternatives, for example, you could use the Rule of 72 to determine how much you can expect each one to make - and by when. This hack can be really helpful when you're trying to meet a specific future financial goal.

Using this little trick, a 6% expected return and a 7% expected return don't look so similar to each other anymore. Neither do 8% and 9%.

Let's dig in and learn the Rule of 72. I like to use it in two different ways:

1. When you divide the number 72 by the expected return on your investment, the result (called the *quotient* in math) is the number of years it will take you to double your money. Let's say you have some money that you want to double in

value over the next ten years so you can use it to pay for your child's university education.

2. You set up a meeting with your investment advisor, explain the situation, tell them you want to put your money to work, and ask for suggestions. The advisor then shows you a fancy brochure with charts, graphs and pretty colors, and tells you that you can expect a 6% return on your investment.

Using the Rule of 72, you divide 72 by six and get the answer twelve. That means it will take twelve years to double your money. Hmmmm, not quite good enough. But empowered by your knowledge and understanding, you can take the next steps: you can research and choose different investments with higher expected rates of return and/or you can commit to saving more money to meet your goal.

3. When you divide 72 by the number of years you have until you need to double your money, you determine the interest

rate you need on your investments. In our example above, if you had ten years to double your money before your child went to university, you'd need a 7.2% rate of return on your investments.

4. However, if you got into saving and investing a little later and only had four years until your child started studying, you'd need 18% return on your investment. That would clearly not be practical without taking a lot of risk. So instead, you could start saving in earnest, look for financial aid options and perhaps even delay university for a couple of years to help you bolster your nest egg.

I love the Rule of 72. I love how it helps you to make informed and empowered choices with your money and your investments. I hope you can see how useful this little tool is.

Action steps

1. Using the Rule of 72, calculate the number of years it would take for your investment to double in value with the following expected rates of return: 3%, 5%, 8%, 10%.

2. Decide how much your investment needs to grow to provide for your family (or whatever purpose you have for the money). You may wish to talk to a financial planner if you're not sure of this.

3. Identify when you'll need this money by.

4. Use the Rule of 72 to identify the interest rate needed to grow your money within your specific timeframe.

Download your free worksheets at https://debbiesassen.com/bookbonuses/.

Chapter 6
How Much Risk Can You Take?
Is Investing Risky?

A big reason that many people either don't invest or delay getting started is that they're worried about risk. When I work with people one-on-one or in my group programs, they often tell me that they're very conservative. The markets make them nervous. They don't want to take any risk.

If this sounds familiar, let's try to understand what you're scared of and why.

When people say they're scared of risk, what they generally mean is that they're scared of losing money. And I totally get that. You don't want to lose money. *I* don't want to lose money. It's frustrating and aggravating. Losing a large sum of money can make you worry about your financial security and stability.

But I disagree that this is why you're scared of investing.

You are *not* scared of losing money. People lose money all the time.

And I'm not talking about a one-hundred-dollar bill falling out of your wallet, over-paying for a new dress, or being cheated by the roofer for your house repair. Those kinds of things happen to all of us.

So what's really beneath your reluctance to invest?

You're scared of losing *control*.

And here's why I say this.

As consumers, most of us buy things that we never - or barely - use. For example, take a few minutes to look around your house. Start with your bedroom, and ask yourself:

- How many pairs of shoes or articles of clothing do I own that I've barely used?
- Do I have any clothes with the price tags still attached?
- Now let's move on to other areas of your house. Check your kitchen, your desk, and your bookshelves too. Ask yourself:
- Have I ever given away things I've purchased because they didn't turn out to be what I expected?
- Have I read every book I've ever purchased? Cover to cover?
- What about a gym membership that was great for two months and then forgotten about?
- How much food have I thrown away because it's gone bad before I used it?
- What about my computer - online courses, music, videos or Kindle? How much stuff is collecting digital dust on my hard drive or in the Cloud?

I'm raising my hand here, by the way. I'm guilty of all of these.

We ALL lose money. All. The. Time.

Personally, I may as well have taken a (large!) stack of hundred-dollar bills and set it on fire. I've "lost" a lot of money over the years.
(deep breath)

But when we pay for consumer goods and services, two things happen:

1. We get an immediate exchange of what we perceive as equal value for our money. Even if we never utilize or get full value out of the thingy, our brains register the transaction as value for money the moment we buy it. And we feel good, even great, about it (yes, even if we feel a twang of guilt about buying another pair of shoes).
2. Also, at the moment in which we're handing over our credit card or pressing the BUY button, **we are in control.** *We choose* to spend money.

And we also choose to not use or use up the items we've purchased.

When we invest money, however, the future is out of our hands. It's unknown. And *that's* what's so scary about investing, especially in assets whose prices fluctuate widely.

People are willing to forgo the possibility of earning a lot of money from their investments in order to maintain control and reduce or eliminate the fear of the unknown.

Our human need to have control - or at least the illusion of it - is very strong. It's one of the reasons that some people refuse to get on an airplane, mistakenly believing that automobile travel is safer than flying.

But I strongly believe that a little bit of understanding about the financial markets coupled with a diversified investment portfolio will help you to actually reduce the risk of losing money.

So let's dive in.

The truth about investment risk

When people say they're scared of losing money on their investments, what they generally mean is that they're scared of (a) losing control and (b) losing money in the stock market. They hear stories from their friends and in the media: people facing financial hardship, downsizing their homes, cutting back on travel and vacations, fortunes wiped out overnight, etc. And it's all 'because of the stock market'.

Recently, I was tagged in a Facebook group for female entrepreneurs to answer a question about investing. The OP (original poster) commented that she didn't trust stocks and shares. To her, they felt like "invisible pie." She likened them to the emperor who has no clothes.

While it's true that the stock markets can be volatile (i.e. fluctuate a lot) over short periods of time (less than three years), they are anything but the naked emperor. And over time, stocks actually become more predictable. In fact, the longer you leave your money in the stock markets, the lower your risk and the greater the probability that you'll earn a handsome return.

Let's look at the following chart.

Best, Worst and Average Annual US Stock Market Returns during Various Periods, 1928-2017[6]

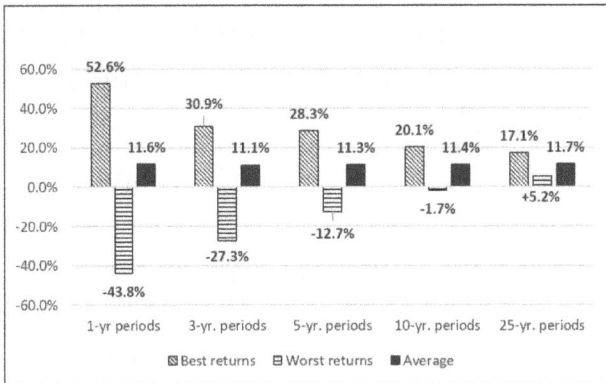

Caveat: because long-run historical information is easily accessible for the US financial markets, I chose these returns to represent all markets. Having said that, financial market returns will vary in

---

[6] Source: S&P 500 Index and http://www.stern.nyu.edu.

different countries, even during long investment periods like 25 years. Past performance is no guarantee of future returns.

This chart shows that in the short term - say one year, three or even five years - the average annual return from investing in the stock market can swing wildly and can be sharply negative. So if you *know* that you'll need your money for expenses in the short-to-medium term, the stock market is not the place to put it all.

As your investment horizon increases however, the range of potential returns narrows and ultimately turns positive - even in the worst case. In other words, the stock market becomes less volatile and more predictable with time. For investors with a very long investment horizon, the stock market becomes a surprisingly safe place to grow their money and build wealth. And as we can see from the chart above, the long-term average return of the US Stock Market is greater than 11%.

Now, let's take a look at the bonds and compare them: I've chosen the 10-year US Treasury Bond issued by the US Government. It's important to note that the interest rates on bonds (i.e. loans) vary greatly depending upon the maturity of the bond (i.e. length of the loan), the credit quality of the borrower and the country in which the bond is issued. The US government is a very high-quality borrower that pays a rock-bottom interest rate on the bonds they issue.

Best, Worst and Average Annual Returns for 10-Year US Treasury Bonds during Various Periods, 1928-2017[7]

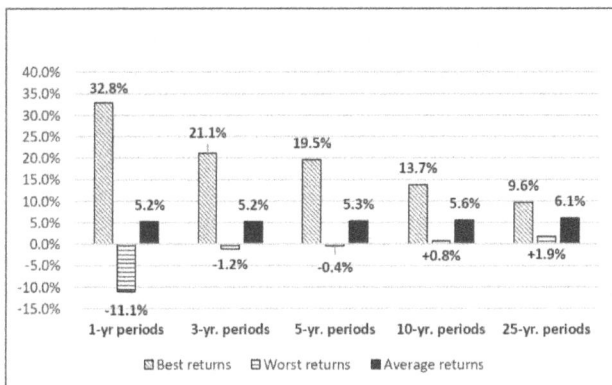

---

[7] Source: http://www.stern.nyu.edu.

The trend here is similar to what we saw with stocks - the range of average expected returns narrows as the investment horizon lengthens. What's different is that the range of highest to lowest expected returns is smaller than that of stocks, meaning that the expected bond returns fluctuate less than stock market returns.

And over the very long-term, the average annual return on 10-year US Treasury bonds is less than half of what you can expect on stocks.

In Chapter 7, I'll talk about how you can use this information to create a diversified investment portfolio.

Choosing the right amount of risk for you

As I wrote above, the thought of investing in risky assets unsettles many investors, especially women. A perceived lack of control coupled with a fear of losing money can make people act more cautiously than they would if they were thinking rationally. And I gave you an example of why, based on market history, it would actually be *rational* to invest in riskier assets like stocks for the long term.

Nevertheless, even with solid and well-substantiated information, there are times in our lives when all of us act irrationally. For example, we:

- Don't get enough sleep.
- Go for days without exercising.
- Eat too much sugar.
- Drive over the speed limit.

If we think about these things for even a minute or two, we might actually admit that those behaviors are risky. And then we'd probably excuse ourselves by saying things like, "Oh yeah, but those are calculated risks," or "Don't worry, I know what I'm doing," or "It's fine, I'm in control."

So now, let's dig a little bit deeper into the concept of investment risk. Let's start by splitting risk into two different categories:

(1) The risk associated with an individual investment or company - called **non-systemic risk**.

(2) The more general risk associated with, say, the stock market, the bond market or the property market - called **systemic risk**.

Note: I prefer to write in everyday language and to stay away from overly technical jargon. However, for this section only, I'm using technical labels to help you differentiate between two types of risk. Doing so will help you to understand and better manage your risk.

Non-systemic risk

Non-systemic risk consists of two components: **business risk** and **industry risk**. Business risk is specific to an individual company, while industry risk refers to the industry in which the company operates.

To clarify, let's refer back to our earlier example of Coca-Cola. As a company, Coca-Cola is risky because something might happen to the company that would lead to losses. They might make a dreadful business decision, face litigation, or perhaps some new research would link Coke to cancer. An example of a bad business decision would be the launch of New Coke in 1985, which was a dismal business failure.

Industry risk refers to an event that would broadly affect all companies in the soft drinks industry, like a massive shift in consumer preferences away from soft drinks and towards fresh-squeezed fruit juices.

You can reduce and manage non-systemic risk by owning stocks in several companies. This is called diversification, which we touched on in the previous section. You can diversify your stock investments by owning several individual stocks. Alternatively, you can buy a stock fund that invests in a large number of stocks. My personal preference is to buy a fund.

Similarly, you can diversify the bonds in your portfolio by buying several bonds or by buying a bond fund. Managing the non-systemic risk of real estate investments, however, is much harder, especially for small investors who lack the money to buy multiple properties.

Systemic risk

Systemic risk refers to the risk connected with a specific type of financial market, e.g. the stock market, the bond market or the property market. Even if you own a diversified stock portfolio, a decline in the entire stock market will affect your investments. Similarly, if the bond market drops due to a rise in interest rates (see discussion in Chapter 4) the bonds you own will also drop in value.

The way to manage systemic risk is to own a variety of different types of investments, e.g. some stocks, some bonds, and perhaps some property if you have sufficient resources for that.

You can't *avoid* risk altogether - but you can manage it

Hopefully you now have a better understanding of risk, why your gut reaction may be to avoid it, and how you can manage and reduce it.

To wrap up the topic, let's highlight three important points:

1. Every choice you make with your money involves *some* degree of risk. Keeping money in 'safe' savings runs the risk that the interest you earn won't keep up with inflation. Investing in an overly conservative portfolio to avoid risk runs the risk that your wealth will grow too slowly. If you're investing for retirement, a conservative investment portfolio may not grow sufficiently large to carry you through your senior years. Investing in a very high-risk portfolio, however, means that a sharp decline in the markets may (a) cause you to panic, sell everything and pull out of the market, or (b) leave you without the money you need at the time that you need it most.

2. You can manage and reduce your risk by diversifying your investments, both within a single type of investment like stocks, and across multiple investment types like stocks, bonds and property. Spreading out your risk means that the collapse of a single company or losses in a single industry or market won't completely ravage your investment portfolio.

3. Investing for the long term - at least five to ten years or more - means you won't be forced to sell your investments at a loss if you suddenly need cash. Having some money in safe savings enables you to patiently hang onto your investments during a market fall, simply riding out the drop and enjoying the rise back up again.

Action steps

1. Write in your journal how you really feel about risk. Has anything that you've read in this book and learned thus far shifted your understanding of risk and willingness to invest in risk(ier) assets?

2. Identify what level of risk makes an investment a no-go for you.

3. Make a note of which of the investments you're considering give you the best long-term rate of return for a risk you're happy with.

Download your free worksheets at https://debbiesassen.com/bookbonuses/.

Chapter 7
Allocate Your Assets

Which assets are right for you?

I've mentioned earlier that diversifying your investments is the best way to manage and reduce risk. You do this by allocating your assets among a variety of investments.

The term **'asset allocation decision'** means choosing the specific way in which you'll split up your investments among the different asset classes, i.e. stocks, bonds, property and cash.

Your asset allocation decision is one of the most important decisions that you'll make for your investments. Your choices influence the level of risk in your portfolio as well as the expected return. Proper asset allocation has the potential to increase the long-term return on your portfolio while reducing its overall volatility, i.e. the fluctuations in its value.

Combining asset classes that move differently from each other (so that some zig when others zag) leads to a less volatile overall portfolio with more stable returns over the long term.

Since no one can predict the future, finding the perfect asset allocation is a fool's game. It's something you'll know only in retrospect - looking back in ten, twenty or even 30 years from now.

That's why I like to keep things simple. **I'm a big fan of the golden rule K.I.S.S. - *Keep it Simple, Sweetheart*.**

For the purposes of investing your first $1,000 or less, I recommend sticking to stocks and bonds. They can be bought and sold quickly, with a small sum of money, and without the intervention of professionals like real estate agents, lawyers and even financial advisors.

To get your investment portfolio going and set your asset allocation, I like the following rule of thumb:

- 110 minus your age = your percentage allocation to stocks.
- 100 minus your percentage allocation to stocks = your percentage allocation to bonds.

The rationale behind this rule of thumb is that we become more risk-averse as we get older. This means that we like risk (even) less as we age, because when the markets fall and our investment portfolios lose money in the short-term, we have less time to wait for the markets to recover and our portfolios to grow again. Therefore, as we get older, it's sensible to shift our allocations from riskier stocks to more stable bonds.

Practically speaking, the rule of thumb works like this. A 40-year-old investor would invest 70% of her money in stocks and 30% in bonds. A 50-year old investor would invest 60% in stocks and 40% in bonds.

"But what if I really, *really* don't like risk?"

I get it: it's exciting to watch your money increase in value as the stock markets rise. But it's *not* a lot of fun to watch your money lose value when the stock markets drop.

And I mean *really* not a lot of fun!

One of the biggest dangers to your portfolio's long-term growth and your ability to build wealth is that you'll panic and sell everything when financial markets plunge.

If investing makes you anxious or you're a newbie investor who's never experienced a market crash, err on the side of caution. Allocate less money to stocks today. As you familiarize yourself with the markets and become accustomed to their ebbs and flows, your ability to handle and manage risk will rise.

Here are two asset allocation rules of thumb for more cautious and conservative investors:

1. Take 20 off the percentage allocation to stocks recommended above. Using the examples above, the 40-year old would invest 50% (70%-20) in stocks and the 50-year old would invest 40% (60%-20) in stocks.
2. **K.I.R.S:** Keep it REALLY simple: create a balanced portfolio of 50% stocks and 50% bonds.

For confident, risk-loving, long-term investors

If you feel comfortable with risk and confident in your ability to stay the course when the financial seas get choppy - which they will! - investing 80% to 90% of your portfolio in stocks might be the right asset allocation for you.

In his 2014 annual letter to Berkshire Hathaway shareholders[8], investing virt-uoso Warren Buffett discussed his best investing advice. This was identical to the instructions he laid out in his will for

---

[8] http://www.berkshirehathaway.com/letters/2013ltr.pdf.

his wife: "Put 10% in short-term government bonds and 90% in a very low-cost S&P 500 index fund."

"I believe," continued Buffet, "[that the] long-term results from this policy will be superior to those attained by most investors - whether pension funds, institutions or individuals - who employ high-fee managers."

If it's good enough for Warren Buffet, it's probably good enough for you too!

The following table lists the four different asset allocation alternatives I discussed above. Since there's no single asset allocation that works for every investor, feel free to tweak these to suit your ability to handle risk and your long-term investment horizon. You may also want to consider asking a financial professional to help you set your initial asset allocation, and to make recommendations for future adjustments.

Investment Strategy	Stocks	Bonds
Very Conservative	20%	80%
Moderately Conservative	40%	60%
Moderately Aggressive	60%	40%
Very Aggressive	80%	20%

Choosing assets

After setting the asset allocation that feels comfortable for you, the question becomes *which* stocks and *which* bonds.

Let's start with stocks.

There are two choices:

1. Invest exclusively in the stocks of your home country, or
2. Invest in the stocks of your home country plus the stocks of companies in other countries.

Each choice has advantages and disadvantages. Let's take a look.

Investing exclusively in the stocks of your home country

The primary advantage of investing exclusively in stocks in your home country is that you avoid exposure to foreign currencies. Exchange rates between currencies fluctuate daily. As a result, if you buy a stock outside your home country in a foreign currency, the value of that stock in your home currency can change *even if its price doesn't change*.

Here's an example. Let's say you live in the United States and buy stock in a British company like British Petroleum (BP). Since BP is priced in pounds sterling, if the US dollar strengthens against the pound, the dollar value of your stock goes down (i.e. your pounds buy less dollars). Similarly, if the US dollar weakens against the pound, the dollar value of your stock increases.

This means that investing in stocks outside of your home country introduces an additional element of risk to your portfolio - the risk of fluctuations in your home currency versus the currency of the country in which you invest.

A major disadvantage to investing exclusively in your local market is that the companies available for investment in your home country represent only a portion of global economic activity and growth. Different sectors make up the global economy: Health Care, Pharmaceuticals, Information Technology, Consumer Goods and Energy, to name just a few. Most countries specialize in only a handful of industries. Investing beyond your borders gives you access to business sectors that aren't widely available in your home country. Sticking to investments exclusively in your home country reduces the diversification in your portfolio, while reaching beyond your borders increases it.

Since no one can predict the future, diversifying your stock investments to companies around the world gives you the best chance of benefiting from global growth.

Of course, the advantages and disad-vantages of option #2 - investing in stocks of both your home country plus the stocks of companies in other countries - are the reverse of option #1. The primary disadvantage is currency risk, while the primary advantage is diversification around the world.

So what should you do?

First things first. It's critically important to invest in the way that feels most comfortable to you. This increases the chance that you'll hold onto your investments, rather than selling them in a panic when the markets drop.

My personal preference is to invest in companies all over the world.

Over the last 50 years, the engine of economic activity has slowly been shifting. In particular, the contribution of the United States to global economic growth has declined, while growth in other countries, e.g. China, is on the rise. A sensible investor who wants a piece of all of the world's growth will divide up her assets around the globe. Under-standably, over the long term, some countries and individual companies will do better than others. But today, none of us knows which ones they'll be. Investing in a global stock portfolio is the least risky way of investing with the greatest possible amount of diversification.

To invest in stocks around the world, you can buy individual stock index funds that track specific regions, e.g. the US, the UK, Europe and Asia. Alterna-tively, you can buy a single fund that tracks the performance of the total world stock market. A benefit of this latter strategy is that your stock investments are simple and easy to maintain - they're all in one fund. You never have to think about which countries or stocks will have better returns in any given year.

What about bonds?

Bonds are the stable part of your portfolio. They provide the anchor when the investing seas get rough - which, as I've mentioned several times now, they will. Adding bonds to a stock portfolio reduces its overall riskiness and volatility. Adding stocks to a bond portfolio, on the other hand, increases portfolio volatility *and* the long-term expected return of the portfolio. The bottom line is that by combining these two asset classes together, you should get a better long-term return on your portfolio, with lower risk. Review the table above for options that might suit you.

I recommend investing in bonds in your home country and your home currency to avoid the risk of foreign currency fluctuations. To keep your risk as low as possible, invest in high quality government bonds.

Some people like to invest in corporate bonds (bonds of companies). But beware that this choice introduces an extra element of risk to your portfolio, since companies aren't always profitable - and some even go bankrupt. It's true that governments can also go bankrupt and default on their loans (remember, bonds are loans). However, if you live in a stable Western country, your government can usually take out a new loan (issue a new bond) to pay back its existing loan. In a crunch, they can always print money.

I prefer to keep it simple: risk on the stock side of the portfolio, stability on the bond side.

If you want more risk, keep it simple. Buy more stocks.

It's not what you make, it's what you keep - costs matter!

As you create the asset allocation that best suits your needs, remember that it's not what you make, but what you keep that matters. For this reason, aim to keep your fees as low as possible.

Here's a list of the most common fees that you might pay:

Investment Management	Charged as a percentage of the total assets under management and paid to the broker or investment advisor managing your portfolio.
Expense Ratio (ER) or Management Expense Ratio (MER)	The annual fee paid to the managers of mutual funds and ETFs, expressed as a percentage of assets under management. The ERs for passively managed funds are (significantly) less than for actively managed funds.
Trading Commissions and Transaction Fees	Paid to your broker for buying and selling assets.
Custodian or Safekeeping fees	Paid to the institution that houses your investments.

Over time, the fees that you pay can significantly impact the amount of your wealth that you keep and grow for the future. Make sure you understand what you're paying for and how it affects the long-term return of your investment portfolio.

Action steps

1. Revisit the information you wrote down in Chapters 5 and 6 about how much you'll need to make, when you'll need it, and what level of risk you're happy with.

2. Add in any unique aspects of your life situation that might affect your ideal asset allocation - for example, do you have children or other dependents, or a business you run?

3. Sit down and follow the steps above to decide on the right asset allocation for you.

Download your free worksheets at https://debbiesassen.com/bookbonuses/.

Chapter 8
Choosing Who Will Help You

Robo-Advisors

When you start out investing your first $1,000 (or less), your choices are limited. Most investment advisors won't make time for you. After all, you'll take up an hour of their day filling out forms and answering questions for your small nest egg. An investor with $500,000 takes the same one hour, but the commissions for the big investor are so much higher.

That's OK though. The investing world has shifted dramatically in the last few years. Small investors are better served today than they've ever been in the history of investing. Dozens of automated investing services have cropped up all over the globe. These services, also known as **Robo-Advisors** or **Online Financial Advisors**, use the latest technology to invest your money efficiently and intelligently at rock bottom prices using market index funds.

For the investor, the process is painless and simple. It takes only a few minutes to open an account online at your computer or even via an app on your phone. You answer a series of questions about your investing experience, the time horizon for your investments, the goal for your money (e.g. retirement or general investing) and your risk tolerance. Based on your answers, a portfolio of Exchange Traded Funds (ETFs) is created by computer algo-rithms to match your investment profile. You then *fund the account* by transfer-ring money to it.

If you have any questions, you can speak with a qualified financial advisor.

To grow your wealth, one of the best and strongest financial moves you can make is to transfer money regularly to your investment account - weekly or monthly automated transfers are best. Start with $5 if that's all you can squeeze out of your monthly budget.

You can also choose to invest 'what you can when you can', but let me warn you: leaving it open-ended usually means it gets forgotten. Automating the process ensures your investing gets done.

Another clever trick offered by a few Robo-Advisors is **the round-up feature**. You connect the investing app to your checking account and credit cards, and the app rounds up the cost of every transaction to the nearest dollar. It then regularly transfers the difference to your investment account. It's a practical-ly painless way of increasing your investments.

For a list of Robo-Advisors in your country, I recommend starting by doing some online research.

In the United States, Robo-advisors must be registered investment advisors, which are regulated by the Securities and Exchange Commission. Ensure that the Robo-advisor you are considering in your country is regulated by the appropriate regulatory authorities.

Investment Advisors and DIY

I know I said in the previous section that most investment advisors won't give you the time of day. But some investment advisory firms enable you to use their platforms to invest on your own. In the US, for example, investment companies like Vanguard, Fidelity and Schwab act as places where you can buy, sell and hold your investments. Similar investment platforms are available in many countries around the world at varying costs.

Before you start DIY-ing your investment portfolio however, make sure you understand the fees involved. In particular, check for the following:

1. Will you be charged an annual administration or safekeeping fee as either a flat fee or as a percentage of your holdings?

2. Will you be charged for buying and selling investments? If so, will it be as a flat fee or as a percentage of the trade value? If you're a 'buy and hold' investor, a flat fee may impact your returns negligibly, while a percent-based charge can add up quickly if you actively trade your portfolio.

3. What's the **expense ratio** (called **management expense ratio** in some countries) on your funds? The expense ratio is expressed as a percentage of assets under management. It includes the **management fee** paid to the professional who manages the fund plus the **transaction costs** - the costs of buying and selling investments.

The expense ratio for the fund is deducted from the return on your portfolio, and the fund manager is required to post returns after adjusting for fees. Note that you pay the expense ratio *in addition* to fees #1 and #2 above.

Choosing the DIY Approach

If you choose this option, limit the number of funds in which you invest. Keep it simple by choosing a three-fund[9] or four-fund portfolio. You can do this without stress by investing in a broad bond market index tracker in your home country, plus two or three broad stock market index tracker funds. That's all you really need to design a well-diversified investment portfolio that you can manage easily over time.

US investors benefit from a deep and well-developed financial market. A three-fund portfolio is easy to construct using market index funds for the Total Government Bond Market, the Total US Stock Market and the Total International Stock Market. Investors outside the US, where the financial markets are less efficient and less well-developed, may need to use two or three stock market index funds to achieve their goals.

---

[9] https://www.bogleheads.org/wiki/Three-fund_portfolio.

Either option is fine. Don't overthink it. Focus on getting started more than getting it right. The majesty of this investment strategy is in its simplicity. As you become more familiar with the markets and feel more confident investing, you'll have ample time to tweak your portfolio.

Special Situations: US citizens investing in funds issued outside the US; Investors living in Israel

As a dual US/Israeli citizen, I have a unique window on the global investing arena. In this section I address two investing challenges:

1. US citizens, both expats like me and US citizens living in the US, are strongly advised not invest in mutual funds and ETFs issued outside of the United States. These investments qualify as PFICs (Passive Foreign Investment Companies[10]) for US tax purposes. The tax treatment of PFICs is unfriendly and expensive. In addition, the annual

---

[10] https://www.investopedia.com/terms/p/pfic.asp

reporting to the IRS is lengthy and complex, most likely requiring the help of an accountant (for several hours of tax preparation services).

While US citizens living in the US don't usually encounter this challenge, those of us living abroad do.

Most US citizens living outside the United States can buy and sell ETFs issued in the United States through (a) their local banks or investment managers, or (b) low cost brokers in the US. The former option is usually more expensive. Two US brokers, among others, that serve the expat community as of this writing are Charles Schwab and Interactive Brokers.

US citizens can also invest in individual stocks and individual bonds issued outside the US since they are not PFICs.

Make sure to consult with your US tax advisor as necessary and appropriate.

2. Investors living in Israel. As of this writing, Robo-Advisors in Israel require a minimum of NIS 25,000 or NIS 50,000

to get started. Unfortunately, many new investors don't have that amount money - including those who want to start with $1K or less. My hope is that with time, 'real' robo-advisors that serve small and newbie investors will become available in Israel, just like in the US, UK, Canada, Australia, and other countries.

Small investors in Israel and those who are just getting started can invest via the local banks, where fees may be high. After amassing your first NIS 20K, less expensive opportunities are available through the local investment houses.

A relatively new investing vehicle worthy of consideration is the *Kupat Gemel le Hashka'ah* (קופת גמל להשקעה)[11]. Investors who leave their money in these vehicles until the age of 60 and withdraw their funds via a monthly stipend (rather than a lump sum) can enjoy huge tax savings.

---

[11] https://goldfus-ins.co.il/en/beginners-guide-to-kupat-gemel-lehashkaa/

In depth information on these investing alternatives is beyond the scope of this book, and may require a meeting with a pension advisor or financial advisor. US citizens should proceed with caution due to the 'PFIC issue' and may need to consult with their US tax advisors.

Action steps

1. Make a list of full-service brokerage firms and financial advisors you'd consider working with. Look at the fees and clarify what services you get in exchange for the fees you pay.

2. Now, make a list of low-cost brokerage firms you could work with, and check out Robo-advisor options. Are you comfortable DIY-ing your investments or is a full-service provider a better option for you?

3. Set up your investment account and get started. Remember: all the research in the world won't replace actually taking action.

Download your free worksheets at https://debbiesassen.com/bookbonuses/.

SECTION 3

MYTHS, MISTAKES
AND NEXT STEPS

Chapter 9
The Three Myths
that Keep You from
Getting Started

So if it's easy, why isn't everyone doing it?

As you worked through the previous section, you might have found yourself thinking, "It can't possibly be that easy. If it were, then more people would be doing it!"

And, of course, the truth is that investing *does* take a little bit of time to figure out - you need to learn some basic financial terms, research a few options and then choose what's right for you. But honestly, I don't think it's a lack of time that keeps people from getting started.

In my experience of working with hundreds of people from several different countries, there are three very common myths that keep them from even realizing that investing is an option for them. Chances are that you've come across one or more of these myths yourself, so I want to spend some time in this chapter acknowledging and then dismantling each one.

Myth 1: You CAN'T do it by yourself

The idea that you HAVE to get professional investing help is probably the Number 1 myth out there. It's perpetuated by constant messages from the media and ads from financial professionals (who, let's face it, have a vested interest in you not believing you can do it on your own).

Plus, as we've already touched on, all the financial jargon and industry terminology can be intimidating. It can leave people feeling like they're incompetent - or at least too financially illiterate to even think about investing alone.

But as I mentioned in Chapter 8, even if you're just starting out and only have a small portfolio to think about, you absolutely CAN do it on your own. In fact, due to the costs involved in hiring an investment advisor, I think you *must* do it on your own. And as I keep saying, investing really isn't rocket science.

Plus, you can be confident that you'll always have your own best interests at heart in any financial decisions you make. Doing it yourself allows you to become your own best advocate.

Myth 2: Someone else automatically knows better than you

The second myth is that a qualified financial professional automatically knows your best investment options - and knows them better than you.

This can be true when that person takes the time to sit with you and gets to know you and your unique situation in depth. When you're clear on your goals, dreams and concerns, a professional investor might know about a few options that you don't.

But for a starter portfolio, the investment alternatives are limited. And that's OK. As you get started with investing your first $1,000, you have an ideal opportunity to learn about investing and commit to the process.

Hopefully you now agree that this isn't so complicated. You absolutely can master investing if you want to. And *then,* once you've grown a nice nest egg by regularly contributing to your investment account and enjoying the magic of compound interest, you can bring in an investment advisor to review your portfolio. They'll be able to spot what needs to be tweaked and adjusted with your investments. They may even recommend something that was untouchable back when you were a small, newbie investor.

And you'll have the choice - and the confidence - to either accept the advice, or walk away.

Myth 3: Property is the only safe way to invest

The third and final myth is that property is the best way to invest for safe and high returns. Hopefully I covered this thoroughly in the previous section. But let's recap.

First, like any financial market, the property market has cycles too. Sometimes the market rises and sometimes it falls, just like the stock market. In addition, you can miss earning rental income during periods when you don't have tenants. And if the plumbing or air conditioner needs to be repaired, you can end up funneling more money back into your investment property than you're taking out. Property investments require time, energy, and cash from time to time. You can't simply buy a property, then 'set it and forget it' like you can with a diversified investment portfolio.

Does that mean you should abandon the idea of property altogether? Absolutely not. But you *do* need to go into property investing with your eyes wide open.

Remember too that property isn't a liquid investment type. That means that if you need cash quickly, you can't sell it in a hurry, unlike stocks and bonds. If the property market's in bad shape, it can take months - or even years - until a buyer comes along.

So go ahead and invest in property - but do so as *part* of a well-diversified investment portfolio.

Chapter 10
Investing Mistakes
to Avoid

It might not be rocket science, but there ARE a few watch-outs

As I've said throughout this book, I firmly believe that investing is easier than most of us think. Nevertheless, there are a few mistakes I regularly see people making, and I want you to bypass them. These mistakes are incredibly easy to avoid, so I'm sharing them with you now to help prevent you from making them on your own investment journey.

Mistake 1: Waiting to get started

There's a well-known saying that if you want shade, the best time to plant a tree is 20 years ago. Failing that, the second-best time to plant is right now. And nowhere is that truer than with investing. The magic of compound interest, which I discussed in Chapter 5, is a mind-boggling phenomenon.

Remember our friend Irene who started investing $100 a month from the age of 25? Her wealth grew to over $500,000 by the time she reached 70. But what would have happened if Irene had waited 10 years to get started? Perhaps she was busy with school, starting a business, her family and more, so she didn't get her act together until she hit 35. No problem, you say. Irene still invests $100 a month for the next 35 years. So her total principal is $42,000 instead of $54,000. How much of a difference can that make?

How MUCH of a difference can that make?

A lot!

In this case, Irene's wealth will grow to only $224,500 - a difference of $277,500 because she got started ten years later.

And if you think that investing $200 a month for 35 years will close the gap, think again. In that case Irene will have only $458,770 when she retires.

As an alternative, let's say that Irene gets started investing at age 25. She invests for ten years and then discovers she can't keep up. Her family has grown. She's living paycheck to paycheck, barely treading water, and she now needs every single cent. So at age 35, Irene stops adding new money to her investment account.

How much will she have in her account at age 70? **$277,500!**

Irene's ten years of investing as a young adult are worth more than 35 years of investing later on.

Again, *that's* the magic of compound interest.

Now, I don't want you to get frustrated, chuck in the towel and resign yourself to believing that you've waited too long. If I put you in a room filled with diamonds and told you to grab as many as you could for the next five minutes, you wouldn't waste your time complaining that you need ten minutes. You'd start stuffing your pockets as quickly as possible, right?

Compound interest is waiting for you. Start filling your pockets now!

Mistake 2: Putting all your eggs in one basket

People are always looking for the next high flyer. They've watched Apple soar by about 1,000% over the last ten years and now *they* want a piece of the action too. So they try to pick one particular stock that they're sure will take off in the same way, and then bet everything on it, only to lose it all…

I've already talked extensively about the importance of diversifying your portfolio to lower your risk back in Section 2. So I won't repeat that all again here. Instead, I'll simply remind you that the smart way to invest involves spreading out your eggs.

Don't bet on a single race horse, a single property or a single promising start-up. Understand your tolerance for risk, and diversify your portfolio accordingly.

Mistake 3: Not being tax-smart

Most people forget that taxes can significantly impact their investment returns. If your goal is to invest for the long term, e.g. for your retirement, make sure to use *all* the tax advantages to which you're entitled. Also ensure that you invest using a recognized pension, IRA or super account (whichever is relevant in your country).

In the US and many other countries, you can use the tax code to your benefit (even if your investments are held in taxable accounts) to offset any gains with losses.

Make sure to consult with an accountant *before* you start investing. Find out what you need to know to legally avoid paying more tax than you need to.

Conclusion
Where to From Here?

You've learned a lot about investing in this little book

As you've travelled through the pages of this book with me, you've learned quite a bit about getting started with investing. You've learned that:

- You don't have to have hundreds of thousands of dollars to get started: $1,000 - or less - is enough.
- You do however, need to get started as soon as possible to benefit from the power of compound interest.
- Saving is different from investing - and you need both.

- Stocks, bonds and property are the three most common types of investments.
- Mutual funds and ETFs are collective investments in which investors' money is pooled in order to purchase a variety of investment alternatives.
- Funds can be actively or passively managed; and research shows that investing in passively managed funds that track broad market indexes will beat actively managed funds at least 80% of the time.
- You can easily follow my simple, four-step process for starting to invest with as little as $1,000.
- There are three persistent myths that you don't have to believe, and three common investing mistakes that you don't have to make!

So you're now probably feeling one of three things...

Excited and chomping at the bit

If this is you, then you're TOTALLY ready to take your first steps toward becoming a $1K (or more) investor.

If that's the case, congratulations: it means this book has done everything for you that I'd hoped it would when I wrote it. All that's left for me to do now is to wish you the very best on your investing journey. Please don't hesitate to drop me a line at the contact details below at any point in the future to let me know how you're doing - I absolutely adore hearing from my readers.

A little bit nervous and wanting to learn more

If this is you, then you've read what I've written and realized that investing IS simpler than you thought it was... but you still don't feel quite ready to make a go of it on your own. If that's the case, it's OK. Seriously. Be gentle with yourself. Everyone's path is different.

And the good news is that help IS available. I have a self-study course called *Investing Made Simple* that you can work through at your own pace in your own space. Most people take eight weeks to go through it, but you can complete it more quickly or more slowly - whatever works best for you.

In addition to giving you the practical investing skills that set you up for success, the course dives deep into your money mindset. It helps you to address your fears, limiting beliefs and re-sistance to risk so you can forgive yourself for past money mistakes and invest with confidence.

You can find out more about *Investing Made Simple* at http://debbiesassen.thinkific.com/courses /investing-made-simple.

Like you'd really prefer one-to-one help

If you've read the book and still feel like you can't quite get your head around the idea of managing your investments yourself, that's also OK. Again, everyone's on their own path.

I'm here to help with personalized one-on-one support. I've worked with hundreds of people - both in person and in my courses - who wanted to ditch financial stress, get out of overwhelm, and become confident money managers. I've helped them discover how to use their money to grow their wealth and take care of themselves by investing for the future and spending on things that really, really matter to them. That means they become calmer and happier, and have more peace of mind.

So wherever you're starting out, I'm confident that I can help.

Reach out to me at debbie@debbiesassen.com.

Let's set up a time to chat. I'd love to see how I can support you.

A few words from people I've worked with

"I'm an intelligent woman with a PhD who's managed multi-million-dollar budgets... But somehow, when it came to my own finances, I was paralyzed by anxiety. Debbie gave me a safe, non-judgmental place to let go of my fears and money blocks.

We worked together for three years until I finally felt that I could do this money stuff on my own. I have nothing but praise for the warm, gentle way Debbie held my hand and supported me to take control of my money."

Judith Segal, PhD | Librarian, Library Director and Artist

"Before I met Debbie, I bounced around from advisor to advisor. Then I attended one of Debbie's retirement planning workshops and knew she was someone who could speak my language, understand my fears and meet me at my level.

We've looked at everything in my financial life. Debbie really gets this stuff and she has helped me move past my anxiety and get a handle on my money. She brings integrity and passion to her work (and she laughs at my jokes!) I feel so much lighter and in control having her on my side."

Dvorah Birnbaum | Architect

"I spent a lifetime immersed in exciting work and never paid attention to managing the money that came in. I always made enough for my lifestyle, and it never seemed important to involve myself beyond simply saving. As a result, I moved into my 60s with limited financial knowledge, skill and ability, and a growing anxiety about whether I'd saved enough and what to do for my retirement.

I am so grateful to have found Debbie, who combines practical and technical knowledge with large doses of encouragement as well as guidance. With her assistance, I identified a range of opportunities, established goals, and now have a working plan that meets my needs. I feel a new sense of confidence and direction in an area that had seemed overwhelming and beyond my grasp."

Naomi Nobel | International Consultant

"Debbie is an incredibly wise and compassionate person whose non-judgmental, simple, common-sense approach to financial management together with her heart of gold is an unusually special combination. I walked out of our session totally feeling empowered and understood.

If I could, I'd tell every woman, in any life situation, 'go and treat yourself to a session with Debbie Sassen' because I know they'll be better because of it."

Malka | Nutritionist

"Debbie worked with us to create a comprehensive, long-term financial plan. From the first phone call and in-depth meeting, through many emails and plan iterations, she was a pleasure to work with. She impressed us with her broad and expert knowledge, her ability to listen and understand the underlying meaning as well as the minute details, and her insight.

She was patient and professional throughout, and she was always willing to research new ideas and options. I am confident that the plan we arrived at will provide us a sound basis for action, and we certainly could not have come close without her help."

Belinda Gerber | Strategic Marketing Communications Consultant and Marketing Copywriter

It's up to you now

You've reached the end of *The $1K Investor*. Congratulations!

I really hope the information in it has been useful to you.

But more than that, I hope this book has encouraged you to believe that investing is something that's there for the taking. I hope you've realized that you too can become a confident investor - whether on your own, or with professional help.

My prayer is that this book inspires you to act.

In fact, before we close, let me leave you with one more wise saying: "It's not what you know that matters. It's what you DO with what you know."

The best book in the world won't help you to take care of yourself and your family financially unless you act on the information within it.

You have all the information you need now.

The next step is up to you.

All my love,

Debbie

Lightning Source UK Ltd.
Milton Keynes UK
UKHW021954220522
403354UK00006B/617

9 780578 474724